The
K
Toddler Book

A Dorling Kindersley Book

100 ways to keep your toddler smiling

Introduction

quiet times

including: • relaxed mornings and evenings • enjoying books and photos

energy busters

including: • party fun • rough and tumble • action rhymes • ball games and pillow fights

pretend play

including: • dressing up, dancing and movement • helping with chores in the house and garden • looking after a play pet • putting teddy to bed

out and about

including: • puttering in the garden • growing a sunflower • going for a nature walk • visiting the zoo • fun in the rain • choosing a pet

things to make

including: • baking play dough and making models from junk • creating amazing masks, hats, and crazy faces • puppets, printing, and painting

food fun

Ideas 26-28 and 60-71

including: • den and picnic food
• popsicles, ice cream, and drinks

toys and games

*Ideas 3-5, 7, 15-19, 81,
85, and 93*

including: • ride-on and pull-
along toys • ideas for partytime
or anytime • games to feed her
imagination

Action rhymes to
enjoy together

Acknowledgments

Dorling Kindersley

LONDON, NEW YORK, SYDNEY, DELHI,
PARIS, MUNICH, and JOHANNESBURG

Senior Managing Art Editor Lynne Brown
Senior Managing Editor Corinne Roberts
Art Editor Glenda Fisher
Project Editor Valerie Kitchenham
DTP Designer Rajen Shah
Production Joanna Bull

Published in the United States by
Dorling Kindersley Publishing, Inc.
95 Madison Avenue, New York,
New York 10016

First American Edition
2 4 6 8 10 9 7 5 3 1

A CIP catalog record for this book is available
from the Library of Congress.

ISBN 0-7894-5951-5

Reproduced by Colourscan, Singapore.
Printed and bound by
South China Printing Co. Ltd

see our complete catalog at
www.dk.com

Introduction

Every day, thousands of people experience the thrill of becoming parents to a little bundle of joy who'll bring them no end of fun. And for those parents, a prime concern will be to ensure their baby remains healthy and happy, nurtured by an environment that offers limitless opportunities for development through learning and play.

This is where *The Happy Toddler Book* can help. Packed with 100 ideas for keeping a baby amused and occupied, it is designed to inspire parents, grandparents, aunts, uncles, and caregivers alike.

Divided into easy-reference sections according to age suitability, the 100 ideas and activities you'll find in *The Happy Toddler Book* will take you and your toddler from his first hesitant steps through to the fun and games of the early preschool phase. And, although the ideas are all lighthearted and fun, where appropriate we incorporate information on how they may encourage your baby's development.

We've all sorts of tips for happy times — from picnics and parties to baking and painting; from fun action rhymes and imaginative pretend play to creative makes using household junk and easy-to-do nature projects designed to give your toddler green fingers.

All of the ideas you'll find in *The Happy Toddler Book* are based on good common-sense parenting. And, while there may be some you will have already thought of, we hope there will be many times when you'll be glad for the inspiration our 100 ideas provide to try something new to stimulate your toddler.

So, why not turn the page and take a look? With its handy mini size, *The Happy Toddler Book* provides you with a source of in-pocket entertainment you can take anywhere and, hopefully, dip into before that bottom lip starts to wobble!

PS If you've forgotten the words of your nursery rhymes, don't worry. Turn to the back of the book, where we've put together a collection of action-rhyme favorites.

The fun

starts here...

1

rise and shine

Your toddler's mood first thing in the morning can determine
how the rest of her day develops. Whenever you can it's a
good idea to make the effort to get things off to a leisurely –
and therefore less stressful – start. It might sound impossible,
particularly if you both have to be out of the door by 8:00 am,
but if you can get up twenty minutes earlier you will find it
pays dividends. Use the time to snuggle up together in your
nightgowns and have a chat or play with teddies. A gentle
start gives you special time together and leaves you both
in a positive mood to face the day.

2

let him do it himself

Your toddler wants to do it and to do it now, *by himself*. So, on days when you don't have to rush out anywhere, let him dress himself. It doesn't matter if his top is on backward or he's wearing odd socks – you can perfect his high-fashion look later! Instead, share in his triumph at having negotiated tricky arm holes.

3

give him a pull toy...

A pull-along toy goes where you go – it stops when you stop, like a very obedient pet. Your toddler will revel in his power over cause and effect. He pulls, the toy follows, and it makes a satisfying noise. Above all, the toy is your child's companion as he toddles about his business.

4

...and his own set of wheels

As soon as he can sit safely astride one, a ride-on toy is a must for a toddler with places to go – it is sure to become one of his favorite toys. Small wooden trikes are a good start, so that your toddler can propel himself along with his feet. When he is older he will be able to master a real trike with pedals. Good exercise for him – and for you as you race to catch up!

5

let him bash...

...with a hammering toy. It will use up some of that excess energy and it's a great way to improve your toddler's manual dexterity and hand-eye coordination, even if it is a bit tough on your nerves! This activity is shape-sorting with a difference – while your toddler learns to match the holes with the shapes, he has the satisfaction of bashing out lots of noise.

6

bake play dough

You will need: 1 teacup of plain flour; 2 tsp cream of tartar;
½ teacup of salt; 1 tbsp vegetable oil; 1 teacup of water; a few
drops of food coloring. Mix together the dry ingredients, then
add the oil. Mix well, then add the water. When you have a
smooth paste, add the coloring. Heat the mixture in a pan until
it is doughy and comes away from the sides. Let it cool and then
knead before using. Store, covered, in the fridge.

play

smiling

sad

surprised

copycat faces

laughing

excited

cheeky

Make an amazing mask from...

8

a paper bag

Start by holding a paper bag up against your toddler's head. Mark where her eyes are in relation to the bag, then take the bag away *before* cutting out small eye holes. Help your toddler to paint the bag with a funny face, sticking on hair and ears if you want to.

a paper plate

Take a paper plate, cut out eye holes, and help
your toddler to decorate it with a face. If you prefer, cut out
a half mask (as shown above). Attach an elastic
headband, so the mask is easy to wear.

bright tissue paper

With a paper plate as the base, your toddler can have great fun
creating a tissue-paper mask. Cut out a nose or beak from card
and glue it on. Make eye holes and add an elastic headband.

paint a crazy face

Just like dressing up, having her face painted lets your toddler adopt a disguise and means she can explore different feelings as she pretends to be a cat, a clown, or a superhero. You will need to decorate her face for her using special face-painting makeup sticks that are available from most toy shops and toy superstores. Don't feel the need to attempt too ambitious a design – your toddler will be just as thrilled with something simple. For extra fun, buy some face glitter and experiment with adding some sparkle to your range of funny faces.

12

make him king for a day...

Perfect for a party or for the dressing-up box, a crown is easy
to make. Take a band of cardboard – if it has a metallic finish,
so much the better – about 6in (15cm) wide that fits around
your child's head. Cut deep "V" shapes into it to create points.
Paint gold, if needed, and finish with jewel shapes cut from foil.

13

...or a wonderful wizard

Measure around your child's head with string. Lay string in a
curve on black construction paper; trace curve with a pencil.
Measuring up from either end of this curve, draw two lines to
meet in a point. Cut out the fan shape you've made. Fold into
a cone; stick with adhesive tape. Decorate with moons and stars.

go clowning around!

A giant pair of clown's trousers will make a comical addition to your toddler's dressing-up box. Go to a garage sale or charity shop and find a pair of trousers, the brighter the better, with a very large waist. Then sew a hoop into the waistband and roll up the bottoms. A wide pair of suspenders will add an authentic final touch.

You don't have to

party to play...

pin the tail on the donkey

All you need is a blackboard or a large sheet of paper with a donkey, or any other favorite animal, drawn on it. Cut out a tail and put a piece of adhesive tape on the back. Blindfold your toddler with a scarf, then ask her to stick on the tail.

16

paperchain congas

Take a piece of paper and fold it concertina-style, until you've used up the whole sheet and have a rectangle of layers. Using scissors, cut leg shapes out of the bottom edge of the rectangle, arm shapes out of the sides, and a head out of the top. Unfold to show your toddler the conga line of paper people!

17

follow the leader

This is a case of the more the merrier, but you can play with as few as two toddlers if you like. Put on some fun music and watch the followers copy whatever the leader does.

18

what's in the package?

Wrap up half a dozen or so familiar household objects using paper and string, then ask your toddler and her friends to guess what each one is. For the sake of variety, make some objects easy to work out and others more of a challenge.

pass the package!

With this game, it's the fun of unwrapping that is appealing. Wrap the prize in layers of paper, pass around to music, then whoever has the package when the music stops gets to unwrap a layer. Keep going until finally the gift is revealed.

20
make her star

Conjure up a magical star and moon theme party for your toddler and friends. Make decorations (like those shown here) from gold and silver paper. Take a length of cardboard that fits around your child's head and glue to make a headband –

of the show

attach a star or moon to the front and repeat to make party
hats for all the guests. Make magic wands from lengths of
dowelling with paper stars glued on the end. And serve
sandwiches and cookies cut using a star-shaped pastry cutter.

Use household
junk to make...

21

...a pair of
binoculars

Collect cardboard packets and tubes,
egg cartons, and plastic bottles and,
with your help, your toddler can create
junk models. Make binoculars by gluing
two toilet-paper tubes to either side of
disks of glued-together thick cardboard.
Create hand-grips from corrugated
paper and a neck-strap from string.

22 ...giant shakers

Using poster paint mixed with craft glue, decorate two large empty plastic bottles with crazy patterns. Let the paint dry, pour in some dry rice, secure the bottle tops, and get shaking!

23 ...a space rocket

Paint a cardboard tube a solid color, then add a door and some windows. Cut out a circle of cardboard, cut into the central point, and fold into a cone; glue. Stick the cone on top of the rocket body. Glue red tissue paper engine flames around the rocket base. You have liftoff!

24 ...a sports car

Let your toddler live life in the fast lane! Get hold of a
suitably large cardboard box and then have fun together
customizing it. Use paper plates for wheels, foil pie dishes
for mirrors and headlights,
and attach a toy or home-
made steering wheel. Pop
a small chair inside and
she'll be off...

25 ...a secret den

Choose a very large box and cut out windows for your
toddler to peep through – you could even glue on squares of
material to make window and door curtains. For extra special
fun, serve up the following delicious
snacks for in-den dining…

26

funny face snack

Den food should be fun to eat. Top a pizza base or omelette with sieved tomato and cheese, and decorate with a silly face.

27

chunky cheese straws

Roll out some puff pastry; brush with egg. Sprinkle cheese over half the pastry, fold to make a "sandwich," roll flat; brush with egg. Cut into strips; twist each several times. Bake on a greased tray for 10 minutes at 425°F/220°C.

28

fruity gelatin pots

Make up some gelatin. Pop fruit pieces into the bottom of individual plastic bowls, then top with gelatin. Leave to set.

29

get into the groove!

Every toddler loves dancing, and having a
boogie around the room will brighten up
any low moment. For a real giggle, try
dancing with your toddler's feet resting
on top of your own. See how long you
can keep in step, changing direction, and
going backward and sideways, too.

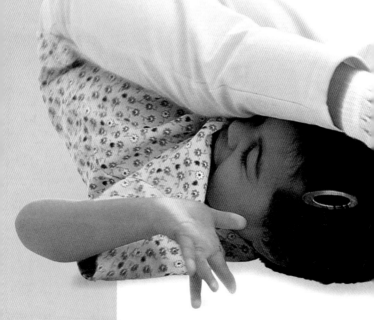

' do a roly-poly '

30

There's no alternative – you'll have to get down on the floor
to show her how to do this one! Don't worry if she can't do
a full roly-poly, it's fun just to try. Whatever you do, never
be tempted to force her over. Every child's coordination
develops at a different rate, so give her time.

put her in the spotlight

For the serious dancer, there's nothing like the romance of the ballet. Whether it's the chance to be the center of attention or just the appeal of wearing a tutu, your toddler will love to dress up and dance. And it's not just the girls, either — boys fall for the glamour of ballet costumes, too. Go with it; it's sheer self-expression.

Heads...   shoulders...   knees...

eyes...   ears...   mouth...

and toes...   knees...   and toes...

32 sing together...

Heads, shoulders, knees and toes, knees
and toes/Heads, shoulders, knees and toes,
knees and toes/And eyes and ears and mouth
and nose/Heads, shoulders, knees and toes,
knees and toes. *And then sing it all over again!*

and nose!

33

play piggy-back

Toddlers need you to direct their boundless energy and love of physical fun. So, get down to their level and give piggyback and horse rides. And don't think this is a game just for dads to enjoy – moms can get involved in a bit of rough and tumble, too!

34
get booked up

Create a book corner, so that your toddler can browse through books whenever she wishes. She's never too young to have stories read to her, but she'll also want to look at books by herself. Books come in all shapes and sizes, with lift-the-flap and pop-up versions being particularly exciting to handle and explore. Your toddler will "read" them aloud to her dolls or teddies, and to herself.

Give

her green fingers

35
water plants

Let her water plants, both indoors and out. Give her her own little watering can to use and be sure to supervise at all times!

37
make a mini garden with her

Give your toddler her own patch of soil to cultivate. Help her plant seeds or make a garden – she'll love it.

36
give her toy tools

A set of mini garden tools will get her digging and raking. **Be careful!** Soil can carry harmful parasites, so keep fingers out of mouths and wash hands thoroughly after gardening.

grow a

cress-head

Take an empty eggshell with the top cut off. Wash it out and leave it to dry. Paint on a funny face. Once the paint is dry, put cotton balls in the bottom of the shell and sprinkle with watercress seeds. Soak the cotton balls with water, put the shell on a windowsill, water every day, and watch the cress-head grow. You will soon be able to give him a haircut!

Wait and watch...

39

...a giant sunflower grow

Plant several seeds (just in case one or two fail) in a medium-size flower pot. Then place a plastic bag over the pot top and fix with string or an elastic band. Put in a sunny spot and tend every day. As your seedlings grow, move them to a bigger pot.

40 ...or a big fat bean

Drop a piece of rolled-up blotting paper into a jelly jar, pop a bean between the glass and paper, and drench paper with water. Put jar in a warm, dark place; water as needed.

...or a curly carrot top 41

Cut tops off several carrots and put these in a saucer, cut-side down. Put the saucer in a windowsill and add a little water to it. Keep wet and watch the tops sprout.

Go for a nature walk and...

"let me help

48 ...cleaning up

With a toy wheelbarrow, your toddler
will enjoy helping you with fetching-
and-carrying gardening jobs, such as
picking up weeds and grass cuttings.

you with..."

49 ...sweeping the path

Toddlers are fascinated by brooms, so buy yours his own mini version. It will be easier and lighter for him to maneuver than a big broom, so he'll feel he's doing a really good job.

50 ...clearing leaves

Your little one will enjoy the challenge of loading himself up with an armful of ever-escaping leaves. Make sure he wears gloves.

51 ...washing the car

You'll need rubber boots, buckets of soapy water and sponges, and rolled-up sleeves! Never leave your toddler alone with water.

let her dress up

With a few props, a toddler can be
anything she wants. Dressing up lets
her experiment with "being" someone
else and allows her to "try out" new
feelings as she plays at being busy or
important, for example. Collect
clothes, hats, shoes, and bags, and
watch your toddler show off her
innate acting skills.

He can help with the shopping by...

57

do the spring cleaning...

...and let your little one help. Even the dullest of household chores looks like great fun to your toddler. After all, she will be imitating grown-up behavior when she offers to "help" you with sweeping, cleaning, or mopping. Give her her own mini dustpan-and-brush set and she will cheerfully putter about, leaving you to get on with your own jobs close by. She'll also enjoy cleaning toy cars with a damp cloth or washing doll's clothes. All the while she will feel she is helping you, too, so encourage her cooperation – it's a powerful antidote to temper tantrums.

58

make her a
mini soap star

Never mind the mess it makes – washing dolls and their
clothes combines several aspects of creative play. Your
toddler will be in her element splashing around in bubbly
water, but she's also copying adult behavior and "looking
after" her toys. And forget any thoughts of domestic
drudgery – for your child this is just good, clean fun.

59

hang out the

When it comes to hanging out the wash, it's very useful
to have another pair of hands to help out – particularly when
they're at such a convenient level for the laundry basket!
Toddlers love to get stuck into mounds of freshly washed

wash

clothes, and unloading the washing machine makes for great fun. Always supervise your little helper's enthusiastic efforts – garments such as pairs of tights and long sleeves represent a tangle hazard and clothespins can pinch little fingers.

60

give her
ice cream...

61

...or whip up
your own

Purée 12oz (350g) strawberries. Add 6oz
(175g) sugar. Whisk ¼pt (450ml) whipping
cream until thick; gently fold this into the
purée. Freeze in a plastic container.

make juicy popsicles...

Toddlers love popsicles – they make the perfect treat on summer days. And they needn't be unhealthy, since you can incorporate fruit juice, pieces of fruit, and yogurt into your recipes. All you need to get started is a set of popsicle molds, some popsicle sticks, and your chosen ingredients. For one-flavor popsicles, just fill your molds with pure fruit juice, squash, or yogurt, put in the sticks, and freeze. For fruit-filled versions, half-fill the molds with juice or squash and freeze. Next, add some fruit, fill with the rest of your base juice, add popsicle sticks, and pop in the freezer again.

63

...or a fruit smoothie

To make a smoothie all you need is milk, some fruit – such as strawberries – and natural yogurt. Blend in a food processor. Add honey to taste and a little milk to thin, if needed. For a really creamy drink, add vanilla ice cream to the initial mix.

64

whip up a milkshake

For a less rich but still nutritious drink, make a milkshake. It's packed with calcium, protein, and, if you use fruit, vitamin C. Just blend together milk, soft fruit, and, if desired, a little honey or sugar to taste. Then pop in a drinking straw and decorate the glass with a slice of fruit. Chocolate or instant malted drink powder are other tasty alternatives to try.

65

go off on a picnic

Having a picnic is a great way to spend an afternoon. You don't have to travel – just going into the backyard with a blanket or tablecloth is fun. Invite friends and teddies and don't forget to…

...pack some tasty

66

mini quiches

A good cheat is to buy uncooked, unsweetened pastry shells and then to fill them with your own egg-milk quiche mixture topped with cheese and onion, ham, or tuna.

67

pita pockets

Warmed pita pockets make for an imaginative variation on the sandwich theme. Fill them with a combination of flavors to create a really appetizing snack. To keep the pita moist, sprinkle with water before toasting or grilling.

treats to munch on!

68

sandwiches

Sandwiches can be boring or they can be fun – the choice is yours! For novelty picnic appeal, why not use pastry cutters to cut out sandwiches in an assortment of animal shapes?

69

cupcakes

Set oven to 350°F/180°C. Put 15 paper wrappers on a baking tray and 4oz (100g) each of self-raising flour, superfine sugar, and margarine, plus two eggs, in a bowl. Beat until soft. Bake in paper wrappers for 20–25 minutes. Decorate as desired.

bake a cake together...

Toddlers love to cook – it's something they see you doing, so they want to do it, too. But it's also a satisfying, creative process where they see the separate ingredients magically mixed together and turned into something delicious. Rather than bake for real, you can give your toddler a bowl and some flour and water, and let him create his own blobby dough – after all, it's the messy stirring and shaping that really appeals.

and make some cookies!

Cookie-baking has the added ingredient
of cutting out shapes. Use a
simple recipe and let your
toddler press out a range of
animals with plastic cookie
cutters and then decorate
the faces with raisin eyes.

72

give her a
play pet...

Toddlers often have a natural affinity with baby animals.
If yours is pestering you for a puppy of her own, a good
initial stage is to encourage her to choose a make-believe
pet from one of her selection of cuddly toys. She can "feed"
it, groom it, take it for walks, and put it to bed – all
good disciplines that will enable you to discuss with her
what it might be like to have a real pet around the house.

...then get her

Having a pet can give a young child an opportunity
to take responsibility (in part!) for another living
thing. It provides a focus for young emotions and
your toddler will think of her pet as a real friend.
Before making your choice of animal, take a trip
together to the library so that you can read up on
different pets and what their care involves.

a real one?

go to the

Whatever your feelings about animals being kept in captivity, zoos do give toddlers the chance to experience close up all the wild creatures that appear in their picture books and on television. Use your trip to talk about color, shape, size, and texture. Compare the size of an elephant with that of a tortoise, or a penguin's sleek feathers with a bear cub's furry coat.

zoo!

75

make a paper-plate person

Draw a face on a paper plate, glue on yarn hair, then attach plate to a wooden spoon. Make several to create a puppet play.

76

make a silly sock face

Cover your hand with a sock, pushing it between your fingers and thumb to make the mouth, and attach two sticky-dot eyes.

77

make a glove puppet

Cut a finger-size hole in a table-tennis ball; draw on a face. Make a scarf (and a hat if you wish) from felt. Pull on a glove, pop the ball on your finger, and tie the scarf at a jaunty angle.

Create cotton

78
a slippery snake

Paint cotton spools, add eyes
and a tongue, and thread onto
string, placing a bead between
each spool. Add string loops
to make the snake slither.

79
a jolly caterpillar

Paint spools, sticking paper
antennae onto the head spool
and adding eyes. Paint blobs
on all other spools to make
feet. Thread onto string.

spool creatures...

sing together...

Ring-around-the rosy, [join hands and walk in a circle]
a pocket full of posies.
Ashes, ashes,
we all fall down! [fall down on the floor]

Picking up the daisies, [sit on the floor with hands joined]
picking up the daisies.
Ashes, ashes,
we all jump up! [jump up off the floor]

put together a feely bag

Great for parties or for any time, this is a game that is easily put together and will keep your little one and her friends highly amused. All you need is a pillowcase or cushion cover and a variety of objects to put inside it. Pick items that offer a range of textures for small hands to explore – wooden, metallic, velvety, rubbery, and so on. For shock value and guaranteed giggles, put in the unexpected – try cold cooked spaghetti or a package of frozen peas!

get out the photos

Looking at photos together is a good quiet-time activity, and you'll enjoy talking about the people in the photos as much as your toddler will enjoy hearing about them. Photos make a great talking point and give your child a better understanding of how he fits into the bigger family unit. Show him photos of you when you were a child, as well as pictures of himself when he was a baby.

hand her a paintbrush...

Toddler paintings deserve to command high prices – they're colorful, flamboyant, and big! Encourage your child to paint whenever she wants to and, if you like, why not join in yourself? You don't need an easel – just large sheets of paper, a brush, and child-safe paints, plus plenty of protective newspaper (painting outside is an even better option if you have a backyard and the weather permits). You could always cut down one of dad's old shirts to make an artist's smock – this will minimize paint stains on clothes and allow your toddler to give free rein to her creative exuberance.

...and let him put his foot in it

Let him experiment with foot- and handprints. Girls and boys alike love getting messy with paint but, for the sake of your soft furnishings, always be around to supervise! The bigger the sheets of paper you can get for your toddler to use the better – this way he can create some elaborate patterns. For printing on a small scale, use sponge shapes or potato cutouts.

build his imagination

As soon as your toddler has the manual dexterity and coordination to fit two plastic bricks together, he's off. If there's one type of toy that's designed to have lasting appeal, the humble construction set is it. From towers to traffic lights to trains, he can create whole worlds from one bucket of bricks.

Play ball

bowling

Why not do some bowling? Take several empty plastic bottles and half-fill them with water. Arrange them bowling-style and use a small ball to knock them down.

throwing

By 18 months, your toddler will probably have sufficient balance to throw a ball. Remove all nearby breakables!

games!

88

kicking

Some toddlers are natural soccer players, while others find ball control a little more challenging. A fun kick-around usually goes over well though, but try to keep it gentle.

Go and get wet...

...puddle jumping

Put on waterproof
clothes and boots and go
out together hunting for
puddles. Toddlers love the
sensation of stamping their
feet and watching the water
splash up. And it's a great
way to let off steam!

90

...raindrop racing

Play the raindrop-racing game – all you need is a wet windowpane! Ask your child to pick a raindrop at the top of the glass and then pick one yourself. See which gets to the bottom first.

91

...umbrella dancing

Take a lead from the movies – put up your umbrellas and find an open space (well away from traffic!). Swing your umbrellas around (avoiding passersby) and show off your fancy footwork prancing through the puddles.

get in the swing

Swings are fun, whether you're six months or 60 years old. Older toddlers can make the change from a baby swing to a big swing, but you'll need to teach them how to propel themselves and they'll still need a bit of a push.

give her bags of fun

A toddler loves a container — whether it's a bag, a box, a basket, or a lunch box. She will love hoarding objects inside — packing away her favorite things or clothes for teddy — before carrying them around with her looking very pleased with herself. And it's an activity that will occupy her for ages as she packs and unpacks… packs and unpacks… But beware, if you've lost your keys, check out that bag first — your toddler may have magpie instincts!

plump up the pillows!

There's always time for boisterous play, as long as you're there to supervise and it's not just before lights out. Make sure the hour before bed is spent as quiet time, so your toddler can wind down after the excitement of the day.

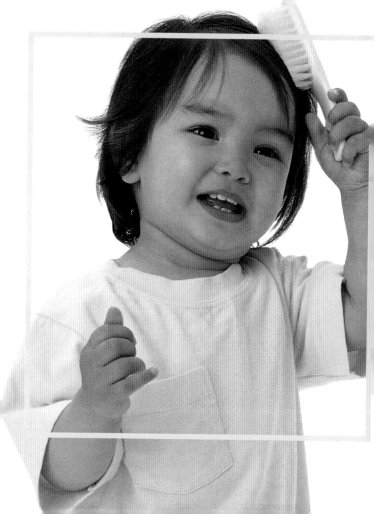

Let your little sleepyhead...

95
clean her teeth

Make sure your toddler's teeth are brushed twice a day. You'll have to supervise.

96
wash her face

Face-washing is never going to be popular, but letting her do it herself may appeal.

97
put on pajamas

Let her try getting dressed for bed – you may well have to help, but resist if you can.

98
brush her hair

Let her primp and preen – it doesn't matter if she goes to bed looking like a scarecrow!

99

...and kiss teddy goodnight...

You can make evenings happier by letting your toddler tuck in teddy as part of her pre-bed wind-down routine. She'll feel very grown-up, and saying night-night to you may be easier for her emotionally if she can relate the idea to her favorite toy.

100 ...ready

for bed

Fun-packed nursery rhymes

Toddlers love singing action rhymes, and even if they can't join in with every movement, the chances are that they'll be happy to try!

These are Grandmother's glasses

These are Grandmother's glasses,
[circle each eye with thumb and forefinger]
This is Grandmother's hat;
[clasp hands over head]
Grandmother claps her hands like this,
[clap hands]
And rests them in her lap.
[rest hands in lap]

There's a wide-eyed owl

There's a wide-eyed owl
[circle eyes with thumbs and forefingers]
With a pointed nose,
[make beak shape over nose using fingers]
He has pointed ears
[point fingers up on either side of head]
And claws for toes.
[make claw shape with both hands]

He sits in a tree
And looks at you,
[circle eyes with thumbs and forefingers]
Then flaps his wings and says,
[flap arms]
"Tu-whit, tu-whoo!"
[cup hands around mouth and hoot]

If you're happy and you know it

If you're happy and you know it,
Clap your hands;
[clap hands in rhythm to rhyme throughout, where indicated]
If you're happy and you know it,
Clap your hands;
If you're happy and you know it,
And you really want to show it,
If you're happy and you know it,
Clap your hands!

The baby in the cradle

The baby in the cradle
Goes rock-a-rock-a-rock.
[rock arms]
The clock in the dresser
Goes tick-a-tick-a-tock.
[wag forefinger from side to side]
The rain on the window
Goes tap-a-tap-a-tap,
[tap finger on palm of opposite hand]
But here comes the sun,
So we clap-a-clap-a-clap!
[clap three times]

Old MacDonald

Old MacDonald had a farm,
E-i-e-i-o!
And on that farm he had some cows,
E-i-e-i-o!
With a moo-moo here,
[make a mooing noise together]
And a moo-moo there,
Here a moo, there a moo,
Everywhere a moo-moo!
Old MacDonald had a farm,
E-i-e-i-o!
*[Also try pigs, sheep, ducks, and
chickens, making the appropriate
noises as you go]*

Old MacDonald had a farm,
E-i-e-i-o!
And on that farm he had a tractor,
E-i-e-i-o!
With a vroom-vroom here,
[make a vehicle noise together]
And a vroom-vroom there,
Here a vroom, there a vroom,
Everywhere a vroom-vroom!
Old MacDonald had a farm,
E-i-e-i-o!

This is the way the ladies ride

This is the way the ladies ride,
Nimble-nim, Nimble-nim.
*[bounce child gently on your knee, getting
faster as rhyme progresses]*

This is the way the gentlemen ride,
Gallop-a-trot, Gallop-a-trot.

This is the way the farmers ride,
Jiggety-jog, Jiggety-jog.

This is the way the butcher boy rides,
Tripperty-trot, Tripperty-trot,

Till he falls in a ditch with a
Flipperty, flipperty,
Flop, flop, FLOP!
[lower child gently down between your knees]

Acknowledgments

Dorling Kindersley would like to thank the following:

Editorial and design
Dawn Bates and Caroline Greene for their editorial contributions, and Elly King, Bernhard Koppmeyer, Sally Smallwood and Dawn Young for their design assistance.

Photography
Andy Crawford, Mike Dunning, Neil Fletcher, Jo Foord, Mike Good, Steve Gorton, Dave King, Trevor Melton, Ian O'Leary, Daniel Pangbourne, Tim Ridley, Steve Shott and Jerry Young.

Picture credits
Front cover by kind permission of The Stock Market.

Nursery rhymes
The editors have made every effort to establish the identity of possible copyright holders for the nursery rhymes featured, but the investigations strongly suggest that the rhymes used are in the public domain.